Instant
Bible Lessons for
Preschoolers

I Belong to Jesus

by Pamela J. Kuhn

Rainbow Books

Rainbow Publishers • P.O. Box 261129 • San Diego, CA 92196

To Maria Stetler, who allows God to develop and use her mind and talents so willingly.

INSTANT BIBLE LESSONS FOR PRESCHOOLERS: I BELONG TO JESUS
©1999 by Rainbow Publishers, second printing
ISBN 1-885358-55-5

Rainbow Publishers
P.O. Box 261129
San Diego, CA 92196

Illustrator: Chuck Galey
Editor: Christy Allen
Cover Design: Stray Cat Studio, San Diego, CA

Contents

Introduction

Do your preschoolers know that they belong to Jesus? It's not just their hearts that they need to give to Jesus, but every part of themselves. After they participate in the activities in *I Belong To Jesus*, your preschoolers will know that their hands, feet, mouth, ears, eyes, personal belongings and life itself should belong to Him. Your students will develop a desire to give their all to Jesus.

Each of the first eight chapters includes a Bible story, memory verse and numerous activities to help reinforce the truth in the lesson. An additional chapter contains miscellaneous projects that can be used anytime throughout the study or at the end to review the lessons. Teacher aids are also sprinkled throughout the book, including bulletin board ideas and discussion starters.

The most exciting aspect of *Instant Bible Lessons* for Preschoolers, which includes *I Am God's Child, God's Servants Teach Me* and *I Learn Respect*, is its flexibility. You can easily adapt these lessons to a Sunday school hour, a children's church service, a Wednesday night Bible study or family home use. And because there is a variety of reproducible ideas from which to choose (see below), you will enjoy creating a class session that is best for your group of students, whether large or small, beginning or advanced, active or studious. The intriguing topics will keep your kids coming back for more, week after week.

This book is intended to add fun and uniqueness to learning while reinforcing what it means to belong to Jesus. Teaching children is exciting and rewarding. In using *I Belong to Jesus*, you, too, will be using your all for Jesus.

How to Use This Book

Each chapter begins with a Bible story which you may read to your class, followed by discussion questions. Then, use any or all of the activities in the chapter to help drive home the message of that lesson. All of the activities are tagged with one of the icons below, so you can quickly flip through the chapter and select the projects you need. Simply cut off the teacher instructions on the pages and duplicate as desired.

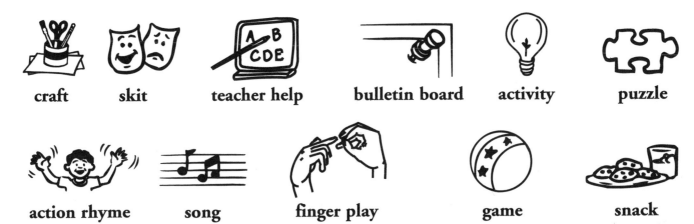

craft   skit   teacher help   bulletin board   activity   puzzle

action rhyme   song   finger play   game   snack

Chapter 1
My Heart Belongs to Jesus

Memory Verse

Let...Christ rule in your hearts. Colossians 3:15

Story to Share
Here's My Heart

Everyone wanted to see Jesus. Word had spread that Jesus was coming through Jericho. Excitement filled the air as men and women tried to push through the crowd so they could be sure to see Jesus.

One little, short man named Zacchaeus tried to push his way through the crowd. *I'll never be able to see over everyone,* he thought to himself. "If only I were taller," he said out loud as people deliberately blocked his way. But it wasn't only his size that kept people from letting him through. Nobody liked Zacchaeus.

Zacchaeus was a tax collector. He was very rich because he collected money for the Romans. Then Zacchaeus would make the taxpayers pay extra to him. Zacchaeus was growing rich because he was cheating others.

Zacchaeus was frustrated when everywhere he turned seemed blocked so he decided to see Jesus another way. He climbed up in one of the big sycamore trees that were planted along the road to provide shade for tired travelers. "Now I can see," he said. Sure enough, there was Jesus walking down the dusty road. Closer and closer Jesus walked. *He looks so kind,* Zacchaeus thought. *I wonder if He would love a sinner like me?*

Just then Jesus stopped under the tree where Zacchaeus was sitting. Zacchaeus was so surprised he nearly fell out of the tree! "Zacchaeus," said Jesus in a soft, kind voice. "Come down out of the tree. I want to go to your house."

Jesus wasn't at his house very long until Zacchaeus knew that Jesus loved him. He was so happy he said, "Jesus, take my heart. I want to belong to You. I will not only give back the money I have taken from people, but I will give them back four times the amount."

Jesus was happy too. "Today a man has been saved!" He said.

— based on Luke 19:1-10

Questions for Discussion
1. How did Jesus know that Zacchaeus was in the tree?
2. Did Zacchaeus' size matter to Jesus? Why?

game

. . . .

Materials
- picture cards
- scissors
- markers

Directions
1. Before class, duplicate, cut out and color in the cards.
2. Divide the class into four groups. Give each group a card.
3. Say, **These cards will help us say the memory verse. The first group has lettuce to help us remember "let." The second group has Jesus, which helps us remember "Christ." The third group has a ruler to help us remember "rule." The fourth group has the hearts. What will that help us remember?**
4. Have each group stand and say their word, filling in with "in your." When finished, the first group's picture goes to the second group and so on. Continue until each picture has been with every group.

My Heart Belongs to Jesus

Memory Verse Review

Christ in My Heart

craft

. . . .

Materials
- hearts and Christ patterns
- yarn
- scissors
- clear tape
- hole punch

Directions
1. Duplicate and cut out two hearts per child. Punch out the holes on each heart. Cut a 12" length of yard for each child and wrap the ends of the yarn with tape. Place the hearts back-to-back and tie the yarn in the top left hole.
2. Give each child a tied set of hearts.
3. Demonstrate how to lace the heart. Help the students tie the end.
4. Give each child a head of Christ to put in the heart. Say, **When you are tempted to disobey your parents, hit your friend, or take something that doesn't belong to you, take the head of Jesus out of your heart and remember: "Let Christ rule in your heart."**

My Heart Belongs to Jesus

finished craft

Giving Hearts

song/craft

. . . .

Materials
- heart pattern
- paper doilies
- glue
- scissors
- index cards

Directions
1. Duplicate and cut out one heart for each student.
2. Show the students how to glue the heart to the doily. Assist in writing their names on the line.
3. Say, **This heart says, "My heart belongs to Jesus." We're going to sing this song and give our hearts to Jesus.**
4. Make a large circle with the children. Sing the song to the tune of "Ten Little Indians." On the last line, have the children lay their hearts in the middle of the circle.

Usage
This song is good for number review. Write numbers 1-9 on 4" x 6" cards. Hold each one as you sing it. You may also give the numbers to the students to hold up.

One little, two little, three little children,
Four little, five little, six little children,
Seven little, eight little, nine little children,
Give their hearts to Jesus.

My Heart Belongs
to Jesus

I Said It!

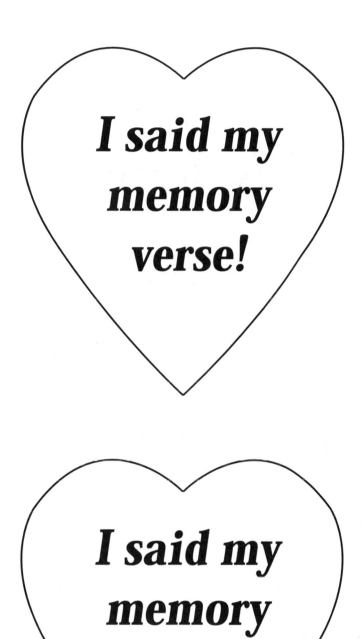

I said my memory verse!

I said my memory verse!

Materials

- heart pattern
- glitter pen
- spring-type clothespins
- glue

Directions

1. Before class, duplicate and cut out the heart for each child.
2. Demonstrate how to outline the heart with a glitter pen and how to glue the heart to the clothespin.
3. Have each child say the memory verse to you. Use the pictures from Memory Verse Review (p. 8) if a child needs help. Clip on the heart when each child successfully repeats the verse.

Usage

This is a good time for positive reinforcement. As you clip each heart to the child's clothes say, **I'm so proud of you for saying your verse.**

My Heart Belongs to Jesus

11

activity

Materials
- activity page
- crayons (optional)

Directions
1. Duplicate the page once for each child.
2. Start the poem with your hands on the floor, then keep stretching and climbing as you say the poem until you almost touch the sky.
3. Start back down slowly until your hands are back on the floor.
4. Have the children follow you with the motions as you read the poem again.
5. Allow the children to color the picture if time permits.

My Heart Belongs to Jesus

Hang On Tight

Hang on tight, we're climbing the tree.

Up, up, up, it's Jesus we'll see.

Hang on tight, we're so high,

We can almost touch the sky.

Hang on tight, Jesus is here.

He says, "Come, have no fear."

Hang on tight, we're moving fast.

Down, down, down, on the ground at last.

My Picture

craft

Here's a picture of me that
I want you to see.
Jesus lives in my heart
and I'm happy as can be.

Materials
- frame picture
- colored pencils

Directions
1. Before class, duplicate the frame for each child.
2. Instruct the children to draw a happy picture of themselves inside the frame and to color the frame.
3. Read the caption to the children.

My Heart Belongs to Jesus

activity

Materials
- heart pattern
- scissors
- brown paper
- adhesive putty
- markers

Directions

1. Cut a tree trunk and branches out of brown paper and attach them to your door with putty. (Grocery bags work well for brown paper.) Cut out one heart for each student.
2. Give each child a heart and assist in writing his or her name on it.
3. Say, **Zacchaeus gave his heart to Jesus. If you want Jesus to have your heart, hang your heart on our tree.**
4. Help the children attach putty to the back of a heart and place it on the tree.

Usage

This is a good time to give the plan of salvation. At this age it is best to keep the prayer short and to the point:
"I'm sorry for my sins. Please forgive me. Thank you, Jesus. I love you. Amen."

My Heart Belongs to Jesus

Heart Tree Door

Tree and Bark

. . . .

Materials

- tree patterns
- scissors
- crayons
- waxed paper
- celery
- pretzel rods
- peanut butter
- cream cheese
- spreadable American cheese
- plastic knives

Directions

1. Before class, duplicate and cut out a tree and trunk for each child. Slit the trunk where shown.
2. Allow the children to color them.
3. Show how to fit the trees together to stand.
4. Help the children write their names on the tree.
5. Ask, **Do you think Jesus ate at Zacchaeus' house? I'm sure Zacchaeus gave Jesus food. What else did he give Jesus?**
6. Give each child a square of waxed paper.
7. Show how the celery and pretzel rods look like a tree and bark.
8. Allow the children to use the spreads on their tiny trees and bark treats.

My Heart Belongs to Jesus

Chapter 2
My Hands Belong to Jesus

Memory Verse

Let not your hands be idle. Ecclesiastes 11:6

Story to Share
Let's Work Together

Nehemiah had an important job. He served wine to the Persian king, Artaxerxes. But Nehemiah was also a Jew and Jerusalem was his heart's home. One day when some men came from Judea he asked them, "How is Jerusalem?"

Nehemiah was sad when he heard their answer. "The people are poor, they are disrespected and the city wall is broken down," the men told Nehemiah.

So Nehemiah asked King Artaxerxes if he could go rebuild the city of Jerusalem. He found it just as the men had told him. Not only was the wall broken, the gates had been burned. It would take many men to rebuild the city but Nehemiah knew that many hands could get the work done.

Each family was called upon to build part of the wall. "Yes," they agreed. "We will help."

The enemies of Jerusalem were angry when they saw the wall being rebuilt. They liked to be able to get into the city and steal the crops from the Israelite people. These enemies threatened Nehemiah and his men. Nehemiah gathered the people of Jerusalem all together. "Don't be afraid," he said. "God is with us and will protect us."

Nehemiah gave some of the workmen spears and shields. They protected the men who were working on the wall. All those hands kept busy for 52 days. Then the work was done, the gates could be closed and guards were posted there. Because of all the hard work, the people of Israel could be safe in their towns and villages.

— based on Nehemiah 1-6

Questions for Discussion
1. Do you like to work together with your mommy or a friend?
2. How can you use your hands for Jesus?

Sing the Verse

song / activity

• • • • • • • • • • • •

Materials
• activity page
• crayons

Directions
1. Duplicate the activity page for each child.
2. Ask, **What can your hands do for Jesus? Look at the pictures and circle what your hands will do this week.**
3. Lead the song to the tune of "B-I-N-G-O."

Let not your hands be idle. No!
Use them for the Lord.
Let not your hands be idle. No!
Use them for the Lord.
W-O-R-K. Yes!
W-O-R-K. Yes!
W-O-R-K. Yes!
Use them for the Lord!

My Hands Belong to Jesus

18

What Is Nehemiah Building?

. . . .

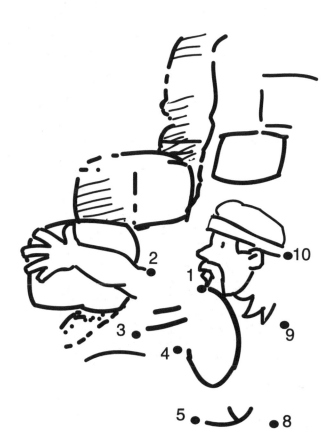

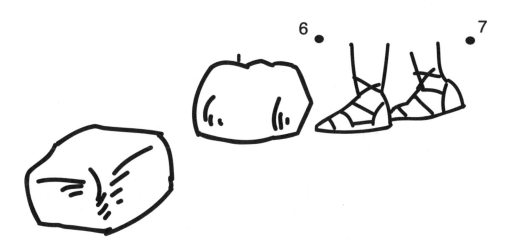

Materials
- activity sheet
- pencils
- crayons

Directions
1. Before class, duplicate the activity sheet for each child.
2. Instruct the children to connect the dots from 1-10. If you are doing this as a class, encourage everyone to start at number 1 and say the numbers with you as they draw from dot to dot.
3. Allow the students to color the picture.

My Hands Belong to Jesus

craft

• • • • • • • • • • •

Materials
- cereal boxes
- spray paint
- label pattern
- crayons
- glue
- construction paper
- safety scissors
- stickers

Directions
1. Before class, cut the boxes as shown and paint them. Duplicate and cut out a label for each child.
2. Give each child a painted box and ask, **Have you heard people say, "I need an extra pair of hands"? That means their hands are too full and they need help. We will make a holder for when you need extra hands.**
3. Assist the children in writing their names on the line. Show how to glue the label to the box.
4. Demonstrate how to trace their hands, cut them out and glue them on the side and around the front of the box. They should place extras inside the box.
5. Allow the children to decorate the box with stickers.

My Hands Belong to Jesus

Helping Hands

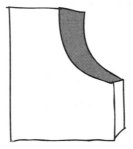

Cut side from box like this.

finished craft

_____

EXTRA HANDS

label

Use Them!

puzzle

. . . .

Materials
• activity sheet
• crayons

Directions
1. Before class, duplicate the activity sheet for each child.
2. Say, **There is a hidden shape in this picture. It is something that Jesus wants you to use. Color the ♡'s red and the ☆'s blue to see the surprise.**

My Hands Belong to Jesus

21

craft

Materials
- hand pattern
- clear plastic lids
- broken crayons
- tissues
- safety scissors
- glue
- yarn

Directions
1. Before class, duplicate the hand pattern for each child.
2. Show the children how to color the hand pattern, pressing down as firmly as possible with a bright color.
3. Demonstrate how to rub the colored hand with tissues until it is smooth and shiny.
4. Assist in cutting out the hands.
5. Allow the students to glue the hand to the lid.
6. Punch a hole near the top of the lid and tie on a piece of yarn for a hanger.

My Hands Belong to Jesus

Handy Reminder

Let not
your hands
be idle

Ecclesiastes 11:6

Building the Walls

activity

Materials
- brick pattern
- children's shoe boxes
- crayons
- glue
- trowel
- bucket

Directions
1. Duplicate the brick pattern for each child and cut them out.
2. Allow the children to color the bricks.
3. Show how to glue a brick sheet to the bottom of a shoe box.
4. Say, **Nehemiah needed help to build the walls. Would you like to help build a wall?**
5. Demonstrate to the children how to dip the trowel into the bucket and spread pretend mortar on a brick, then put their brick on top.
6. Say, **You all worked together to build the wall. It would have been a big job for one, but when you work together the job is easy.**

My Hands Belong to Jesus

A Handy Holder

craft

Materials

- hand pattern
- crayons
- glue
- spring-type clothespins
- magnet strips
- small white paper
- yarn

Directions

1. Before class, duplicate and cut out a hand for each child. Cut the yarn into small pieces.
2. Allow the children to color the hands.
3. Show how to glue the hand on the clothespin and the magnet on the back.
4. Help the students tie a yarn bow around the first finger.
5. Show how to clip several pieces of paper with the holder.
6. Say, When we want to remember something we tie a string around a finger. We want to remember our memory verses. Every time you see this memo holder say, "Let not your hands be idle."

Usage

This is a good way to send home a memo to parents. Simply write the note on the first page of the tablet.

My Hands Belong to Jesus

A Handful of Helpfulness

craft

. . . .

Materials
- helpfulness poster
- watch pattern
- construction paper
- safety scissors
- glue
- hole punch
- yarn

Directions

1. Before class, duplicate the poster and watch, one set per child.
2. Help the children trace their hands on the construction paper and cut them out.
3. Show the students how to glue the hand and watch to the poster.
4. Punch holes at the top of each poster and tie yarn through them for a hanger.
5. Say, Nehemiah and his helpers knew it is always time to work. Take your poster home and when you use your hands for Jesus, have your mommy write the day of the week on the fingers. Do you think you can get all of your fingers filled this week?

It's time to be helpful.

Let not your hands be idle.

Ecclesiastes 11:6

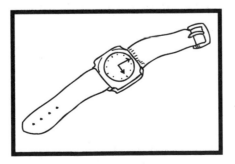

My Hands Belong to Jesus

25

Chapter 3
My Feet Belong to Jesus

Memory Verse

How beautiful are the feet of those who bring good news!

Romans 10:15

Story to Share
I Have Something to Tell You!

"I have something to tell you," said John the Baptist as he wandered from place to place. John the Baptist was Jesus' cousin. God had given John a very important message to tell to the people.

As the crowds sat on the river bank listening to him preach, John said, "What I have to tell you is that you need to get ready. Get ready for the One who is coming soon. Turn from your sin. The Kingdom of Heaven will soon be here."

John's words were different from what the people had heard before. Everything about John was different. He wore clothes that were roughly woven from camel's hair and held together with a leather belt. He ate dried grasshoppers dipped in wild honey he found in the trees. Many thought he was strange, but many believed and turned from their wickedness.

"Repent, repent from your sins," John preached. And as people repented, John baptized them in the Jordan River.

"I'm baptizing you with water," said John, "but this King who comes after me is so good and pure, I am not even worthy to unfasten His sandals."

One day while John was baptizing those who had listened to his words and repented, John looked up to see Jesus waiting to be baptized. This was the One he had been preaching about. This was the King he had said was coming. "I can't baptize You, Jesus," said John. "You are too pure and good."

"No," said Jesus. "My Father, God, wants us all to be baptized to show that we believe in Him."

John obeyed Jesus and baptized Him in the Jordan River. When he did, the sky opened and the Holy Spirit, taking on the form of a dove, appeared and the voice of God could be heard. "This is my Son and I love Him," said God. "He pleases me."

John continued telling others the good news of Jesus.

— based on Matthew 3:1-17

Questions for Discussion

1. Does everyone want to hear about Jesus?
2. Who first told you about Jesus? Make sure you say thank-you to them.

How Beautiful Are the Feet

song

. . . .

Directions

1. Arrange the children in a large circle. Choose one child to be John the Baptist. This child will be in the center of the circle.
2. Hold hands and move in a circle around John the Baptist, singing the song to the tune of "Here We Go Round the Mulberry Bush."
3. At the end of the verse John should choose another missionary who in turn will choose the next one. Continue singing until everyone is in the middle.
4. Duplicate the song to send home with the students. Say, **We have enjoyed singing this song today. You can take the words home and sing it with your family. Make sure all the members of your family have "beautiful feet" for Jesus.**

My Feet Belong to Jesus

How beautiful are the feet of them, feet of them, feet of them, How beautiful are the feet of them who bring good news of Jesus.

Beautiful Feet

_____

will tell
the good
news of
Jesus

activity

• • • • • • • • • •

Materials
- activity sheet, duplicated
- scissors
- crayons
- glue

Directions
1. Before class, duplicate one foot per child. Duplicate the faces and cut out one set for each child.
2. Allow the children to color the faces.
3. Show how to glue a face on each toe.
4. Say, **These smiley-face children need someone to tell them about Jesus. Are you willing to tell them?**
5. Assist in writing the students' names on the line.

My Feet Belong to Jesus

craft

Materials
- feet and tag patterns
- scissors
- poster board (optional)
- 2" pompons
- wiggle eyes
- glue

Directions
1. Duplicate and cut out the feet and tag, one set per child. The feet may be traced on poster board for better durability.
2. Show the students how to glue a pompon to the middle of the feet.
3. Show how to glue wiggle eyes to the pompon's "face."
4. Demonstrate how the tag should be glued extending from the feet.

My Feet Belong to Jesus

Footsie Man

feet pattern

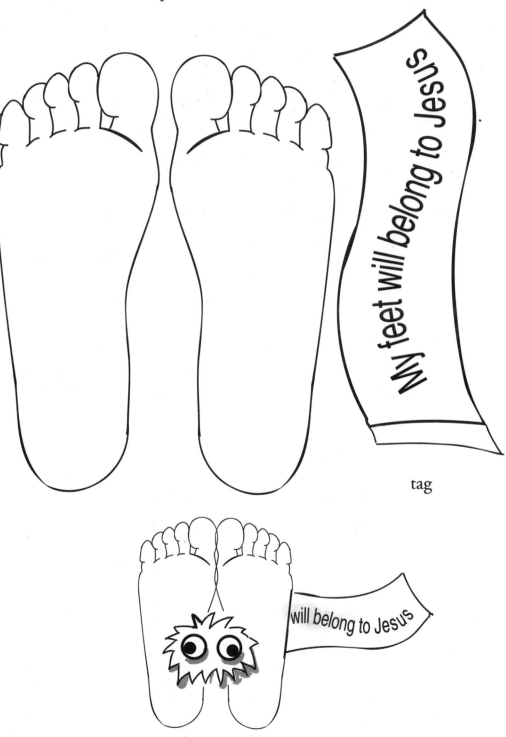

tag

finished craft

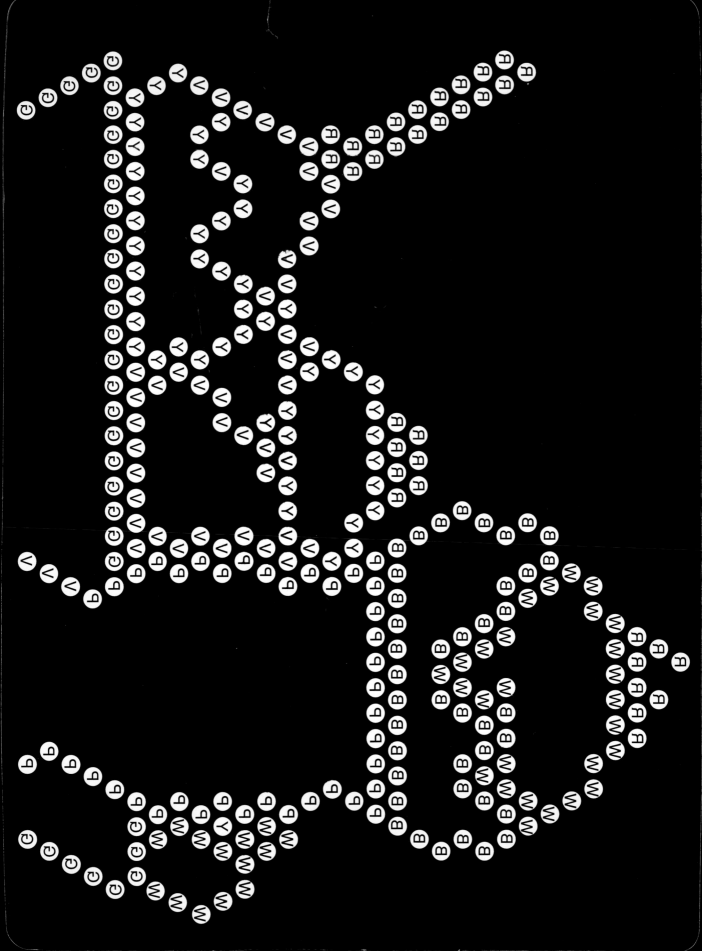

Edible Dough

Recipe for Edible Dough
- 3/4 cup peanut butter
- 3/4 cup nonfat dry milk
- 1 tablespoon honey

Mix ingredients together for a dough consistency. The yield is enough for approximately six preschoolers.

snack

• • • • • • • • • •

Materials
- recipe
- peanut butter
- non-fat dry milk
- honey
- waxed paper
- graham crackers

Directions
1. Before class, make the edible dough. Duplicate the recipe for each child.
2. Give each child a square of waxed paper and a portion of dough.
3. Demonstrate how to make a foot in the dough by making a fist for the foot and making five toes with your finger.
4. Allow the children to spread the dough onto graham crackers for a snack.

My Feet Belong to Jesus

craft

Materials

- John and clothes patterns
- scissors
- instant coffee grains
- 9" x 13" pan
- glue
- shallow bowls
- paint brushes
- clear tape

Directions

1. Before class, duplicate and cut out John and clothes, one set per child. Pour the coffee in the pan. Pour glue into bowls.
2. Allow the students to brush glue on John's coat.
3. Show how to lay the coat in the coffee, glue side down, then shake off excess coffee.
4. Show how to place the coat on John and fold the tabs back. Tape the coat on each child's John figure.
5. Say, What you wear isn't important to Jesus. John wore a coat of camel's hair. But he pleased Jesus by telling others about Him. Jesus will be pleased with you if you use your feet to go tell your friends about Him.

My Feet Belong to Jesus

John's Clothes

Kind Feet

puzzle

· · · · · · · · · · ·

Materials
- activity sheet
- crayons

Directions
1. Duplicate the activity sheet for each child.
2. Instruct the students to color the pictures of those with kind feet and cross out those with unkind feet.
3. Say, **Can you think of a time that you used your feet to be kind? Draw a picture of it in the last box.**

Telling the World

. . . .

Materials
- world and Bible patterns
- Bibles
- colored paper
- crayons
- safety scissors
- crepe paper
- stapler

Directions
1. Before class, enlarge and cut out the world once and the Bible four times. Color them. Freehand cut or stencil the lettering as shown.
2. Assist the children in tracing their feet on colored paper. Help them cut them out then write their names on the feet.
3. Post "We Are Telling the Good News" at the top of the board.
4. Post the world in the center of the board.
5. Staple the crepe paper around the board for a border. Staple a Bible in each corner.
6. Space the feet around the board and staple them in place.

Discuss
Say, If you give your feet to Jesus, when you are grown He can send you to tell others, both near and far, the good news of Jesus.

My Feet Belong to Jesus

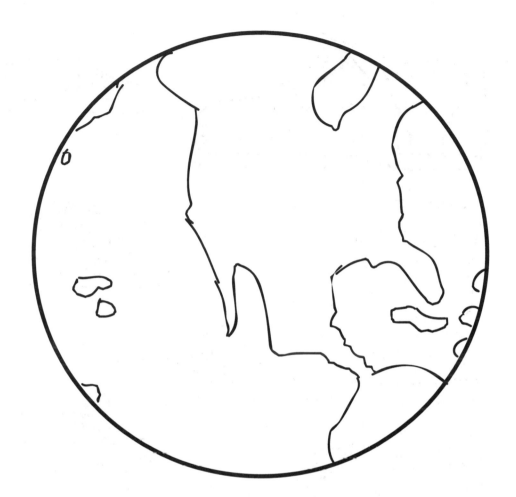

finished bulletin board

Shoe Match

puzzle

. . . .

Materials
- activity sheet
- crayons

Directions
1. Before class, duplicate the activity sheet for each child.
2. Explain to the children how to draw a line from the small shoe to the large one that matches it.
3. Allow them to color the shoes.
4. Say, **Just like each pair of shoes is different, all of you are different, too. You will all tell others about Jesus in your own special way.**

Chapter 4
My Mouth Belongs to Jesus

Memory Verse

Sing to the Lord. Exodus 15:21

Story to Share
A Song Everywhere

Paul and Silas were in trouble! They had helped a slave girl. She was sick. She could tell others what was going to happen to them in the future. The men who owned this slave girl were happy she was sick. They made lots of money by using her to tell others' fortunes.

Paul knew this wasn't pleasing to Jesus, so he asked Jesus to make her well. Once Jesus healed the slave girl, her masters couldn't make money off of her. "I can't believe that Paul!" said one of them. "Me neither," shouted another. "Who does he think he is?"

The men were so mad that they told lies about Paul and Silas. These lies caused Paul and Silas to be arrested, beaten and thrown into prison.

Poor Paul and Silas, their hands were in stocks so they couldn't move. Their backs were burning where they had been beaten. But they weren't complaining. They weren't using their mouths to say ugly things about the men who told lies on them. Instead, they were singing praises to God. Even the other prisoners could hear their praises to God and were touched by the love Paul and Silas had.

Because of the joy they showed, the jailer and his whole house was saved that night. The next day the prisoners were released. They continued to use their mouths to tell others about Jesus.

— based on Acts 16:16-34

Questions for Discussion
1. What does your mouth look like when you aren't happy?
2. What kind of face makes Jesus happy?

activity

· · · · · · · · · · · ·

Materials

- activity sheet
- scissors
- craft sticks
- glue
- crayons

Directions

1. Duplicate and cut out the faces. Glue each one on a craft stick. Duplicate the picture of Paul and Silas, one per child (enlarge, if desired).

2. Say, **Look at all of these faces.** Hold the faces up one by one. Ask, **What does it look like this one feels? What about this one? Paul and Silas need faces. Look at these faces and draw one for Paul and Silas.**

3. Allow the children to color the pictures of Paul and Silas and draw their faces.

Singing Preachers

Paul

Silas

Praise Stickers

craft

Materials

- sticker patterns
- scissors
- crayons
- old newspapers
- glue
- water
- shallow bowls
- paint brushes
- envelopes

Directions

1. Before class, duplicate and cut out one set of stickers for each child.
2. Allow the children to color the stickers.
3. Spread old newspapers on the workspace. Mix 3 tablespoons of glue with 3 tablespoons of water in shallow bowls. Show the children how to paint the mixture on the backs of the stickers. Allow to dry.
4. Distribute envelopes. Instruct the students to keep their stickers in the envelope until they wish to use them.

My Mouth Belongs to Jesus

activity

Materials
- staff and notes
- scissors
- crayons
- glue

Directions
1. Duplicate and cut out the music staff and note, two sets for each child.
2. Give each child two staffs and two music notes. Instruct the students to color the notes.
3. Demonstrate how to glue the staffs together side-by-side, then how to glue the notes on top.
4. Start around the room, taking the first border and allowing the children to help connect and glue the second border, the third and so on.
5. Say, **We will put this border up in our classroom so we'll always remember to sing to the Lord.**

My Mouth Belongs to Jesus

Musical Room Border

Sing to the Lord. Exodus 15:21

Singing Behind Bars

Materials

- Paul and Silas patterns
- scissors
- crayons
- resealable plastic bags
- black permanent markers
- smocks (optional)

Directions

1. Before class, duplicate and cut out one Paul and Silas per child.
2. Allow the class to color Paul and Silas.
3. Give each child a plastic bag. Show how to draw bars on the bag. (Provide smocks to protect clothing while using the markers.)
4. As the children put Paul and Silas "in jail" say, **Paul and Silas used their mouths to praise the Lord wherever they went — even jail!** Let's use our mouths to say "praise the Lord."

Usage

Ask, **Are there places you don't enjoy going? What about the doctor's office? Try praising God for helping the doctor make you feel better instead.**

My Mouth Belongs to Jesus

41

Singing in Prison

song

· · · · · · · · · · · ·

Materials
- handcuff pattern
- scissors
- stapler
- clear tape

Directions
1. Before class, duplicate the handcuffs.
2. Give each child a pair of unfolded handcuffs and staple them on around their arms. Cover the staple with tape to avoid injury.
3. Sing the song with the class to the tune of "Ten Little Indians."

Paul and Silas.
(Acts 16:16-34)

Paul and Silas, singing in prison.
Paul and Silas, singing in prison.
Paul and Silas, singing in prison.
They sing to the Lord.

You can also sing where you are.
You can also sing where you are.
You can also sing where you are.
You sing to the Lord.

I will also sing where I am.
I will also sing where I am.
I will also sing where I am.
I'll sing to the Lord.

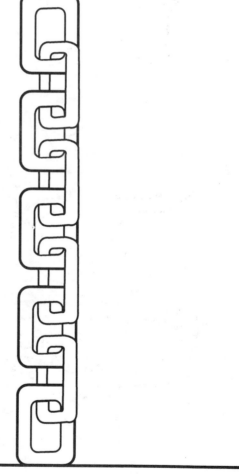

Musical Kazoo Band

craft/activity

• • • • • • • • • •

Materials

- tube wrap pattern
- scissors
- paper towel tubes
- water-soluble markers
- waxed paper
- rubber bands
- glue
- children's music tape
- tape player

Directions

1. Before class, duplicate and cut out a tube wrap for each child. Cut the paper towel tubes in half. Cut waxed paper into 4" squares, one per child.
2. Allow the students to color the music notes on the wrap.
3. Show how to glue it on the tube.
4. Show how to cover one end of the tube with waxed paper and keep in place with a rubber band.
5. Play the music tape and lead the children in putting their mouths over the open end of the kazoo and humming.

My mouth belongs to Jesus

My Mouth Belongs to Jesus

activity

• • • • • • • • • • • •

Materials
- activity sheet
- crayons

Directions
1. Before class, duplicate the sheet for each child.
2. Say, **When you sing praises to God, your heart feels happy. What happens to your lips? That's right, they curve in a smile.**
3. Instruct the students to draw lines from the singing boy and girl to their smiling twins.
4. Allow the students to color the children.
5. Say, When you are finished matching the children, color in the letters at the bottom of the page. It is our memory verse that says, "Sing to the Lord."

My Mouth Belongs to Jesus

Everybody Singing Praises

Exodus 15:21

44

A Heart Full of Praise

Fold paper in half and draw half of the heart on the fold. Cut out.

Materials
- red poster paper
- scissors
- pencil
- music note pattern
- construction paper
- stapler
- glue
- curling ribbon
- glitter

Directions
1. Before class, see the diagram to cut a large heart from red paper. Duplicate and cut out one music note per student. Freehand cut or stencil "A Heart Full of Praise" lettering as shown.
2. Attach the heart to the middle of the board.
3. Give the children a music note and help them write something for which they are thankful on it. Assist in writing their names on the stems.
4. Cut a piece of ribbon and curl it with scissors. Staple one end to the heart and the other to a music note.
5. Lightly spread glue on the lettering and sprinkle with glitter. Attach it across the top of the board.

Usage
The Musical Room Border from p. 40 may be used for the border of this bulletin board.

My Mouth Belongs to Jesus

Chapter 5
My Ears Belong to Jesus

Memory Verse

Everyone should be quick to listen. James 1:19

Story to Share
Can You Hear?

Jesus liked to tell stories. He knew stories helped people understand what He was trying to teach them. One day a crowd gathered to hear Jesus speak. This is the story He told:

"Mr. Farmer was planting some seeds. He had his seed pouch over his arm so he could put his hand in and take out a handful of seeds. Then with a sweep of his hand he scattered the seeds in his field. Some of these seeds fell on the path beside the field. 'Caw, Caw,' the birds called when they saw the seed. They swooped down and ate the seeds on the path.

"Other seeds fell on rocks. They tried to grow, but there wasn't water to give them the drinks they needed. These seeds died as soon as it became hot and they couldn't have a drink. Others of Mr. Farmer's seeds fell into the weeds and thistles. They, too, tried to grow, but the weeds were stronger than the tiny plants. They choked the plants until they died.

"But there were some seeds that fell on good soil. They grew and grew, becoming strong and tall. Mr. Farmer was happy. He had a good crop from the seeds that fell on the good soil."

Jesus told the people, "The seeds in the story are like what you hear of God's Word. Just like the birds took the seeds from the path, the devil comes and steals what many hear from the Bible right out of their hearts. Others hear the Word, like those seeds which fell on the rocks, but when hard times come and things don't go their way all they have heard is forgotten."

"What about the seed that fell on the weeds?" someone asked.

"That seed," said Jesus, "is like those who hear God's Word, but their hearts are so full of the desire to make money, to be better than anyone else, that the Word can't grow. It is crowded out. But there are still more seeds. There are the seeds that fall on the good soil. Some people hear God's Word and keep it in their hearts. They practice the lessons they have heard or read. They repent when they learn they have sin in their heart. Then they go and spread the seed of God's Word to others."

— based on Matthew 13:3-23

Questions for Discussion
1. How should you behave when you are listening to the Bible?
2. How can you put God's Word in your heart?

Listening Ears

Materials
- activity sheet
- crayons

Directions

1. Before class, duplicate the activity sheet for each child.
2. Demonstrate to the children how to match the shadows with the animals and draw a line between them.
3. Say, **These animals all have ears. Our memory verse says, "Everyone should be quick to listen."** Is the verse talking about the animals? **In the box, draw who should be quick to listen.** (They should draw pictures of themselves.)

Sowing the Seed

. . . .

Materials
- activity sheet
- scissors
- crayons
- glue
- round cereal pieces

Directions
1. Duplicate and cut out the bird for each child. Duplicate the farmer picture for each child, enlarging it if possible.
2. Allow the children to color the bird and farmer picture.
3. Demonstrate how to glue the round cereal pieces to the ground by dropping dots of glue on the paper and pressing the cereal into the glue.
4. Show where to glue on their birds so they can eat some of the seed.

Usage
Say, **Look at the bird eating some of the seeds the farmer is sowing. Do you remember who comes and tries to take the Word of God out of your heart?**

My Ears Belong to Jesus

49

Directions

1. Sing the song to the tune of "This Is the Way."
2. Demonstrate the motions until the students can do them with you.

This Is the Way

This is the way we sow the seed, sow the seed, sow the seed.
This is the way we sow the seed, just like Mr. Farmer.

pretend to put hands in bag and spread the seed

This is the ways we shoo the birds, shoo the birds, shoo the birds.
This is the way we shoo the birds, coming for dinner.

shoo away the birds

This is the way we listen to God, listen to God, listen to God.
This is the way we listen to God, listen to God's Word.

cup your ears with your hands

Everyone here should be quick, should be quick, should be quick.
Everyone here should be quick, to listen to God's Word.

snap your fingers with each "quick"

My Ears Belong to Jesus

50

Find the Seed

game

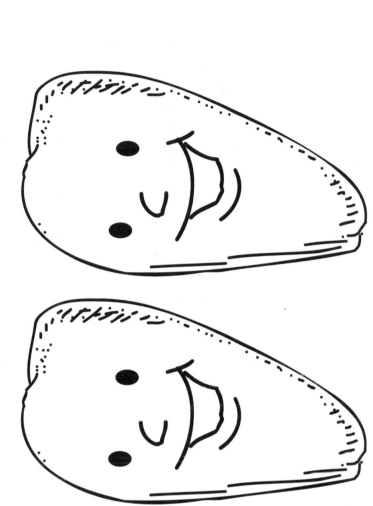

My ears belong to Jesus

Materials
- seed and basket handle patterns
- colored paper
- lunch sacks
- stapler
- clear tape

Directions
1. Before class, duplicate many seeds on colored paper and cut them out. Hide the seeds around the classroom. Also duplicate and cut out a basket handle for each child.
2. Fold down the tops of the lunch sacks three times. Give one to each child and assist in stapling the handles to the baskets. Cover the staples with tape to avoid injury.
3. Hold up a seed and say, Mr. Farmer lost some seeds in our classroom. Let's see if you can find them to put in your baskets. Each time you find a seed say, "My ears belong to Jesus."

My Ears Belong to Jesus

activity

Materials

- bird pattern
- scissors
- toast
- peanut butter
- bird seed
- plastic knives
- crayons
- spring-type clothespins
- glue
- plastic bags

Directions

1. Before class, duplicate and cut out a bird for each student. Toast a slice of bread.
2. Say, **Let's give the birds something to eat so they won't be grabbing God's Word from your heart.**
3. Allow the children to spread peanut butter on their toast.
4. Show how to sprinkle bird seed on the peanut butter and gently press it down.
5. Allow the children to color their birds.
6. Show how to fold the bird in half, then fold the bottom flaps.
7. Show how to glue the flaps to a clothespin.
8. Give the children plastic bags to put their bird treats in, then show how to use the bird clip to keep it closed. Say, **When you get home, take out your bird treat and place it outside for the birds.**

My Ears Belong to Jesus

Feeding the Birds

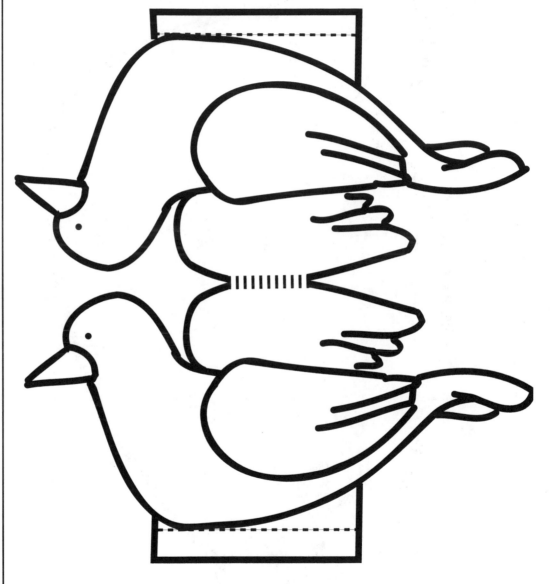

Bird Food Treats

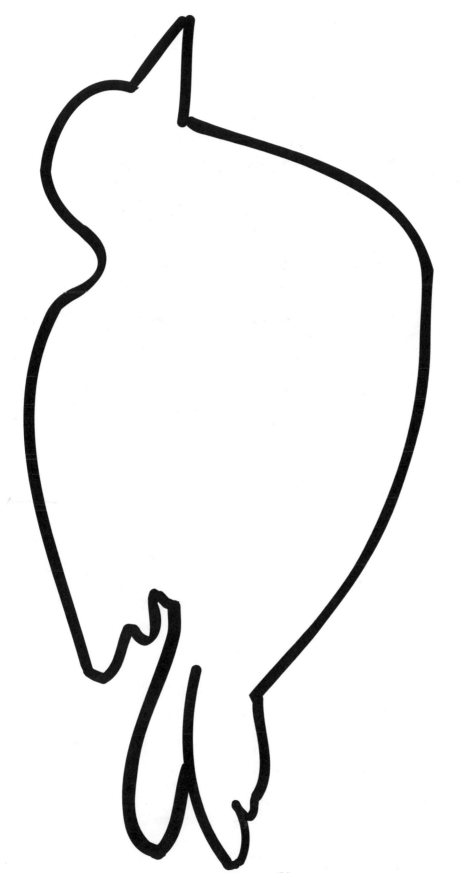

snack

. . . .

Materials
- bird pattern
- scissors
- red felt
- buttons
- glue
- small cups
- water
- crackers
- peanut butter
- fruit-flavored round cereal

Directions
1. Trace the bird on felt and cut out one per child.
2. Show the students where to glue the eye button onto the bird. Give the children cups of water to place on their "coasters."
3. Allow the students to spread the peanut butter on their crackers and add the colorful "seeds" (cereal).

My Ears Belong to Jesus

activity

• • • • • • • • • • •

A Growing Wall Plant

Materials
- plant pattern
- scissors
- crayons

Directions
1. Before class, duplicate and cut out the plant pattern once for each child.
2. Allow the children to color the plants.
2. Have each child say the memory verse, then write the child's name on a plant and post it on the bottom of the wall. Keep adding plants straight up from one another until you form a large wall plant.
3. Ask, **How big of a plant do you think will grow if you listen to and say the memory verse from God's Word for today?**

My Ears Belong to Jesus

54

Add a Plant

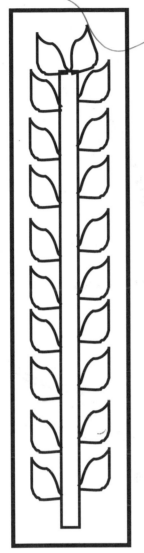

Materials

- farmer and plant patterns
- Velcro™
- flannel board

Directions

1. Before class, duplicate, color and cut out the farmer once and the plants for each child. Attach Velcro™ to the back of each piece.
2. Attach the farmer to a flannel board. Give a plant to each student.
3. Ask the questions, allowing the students who correctly answer a question to place their plants on the board by the farmer. Say, **Let's see how big of a garden the farmer can plant!**

Usage

If you need more questions, repeat these ten. Repetition will help to reinforce the truth of the lesson.

Questions

1. Who should be quick to listen to God? *everyone*
2. What was Mr. Farmer doing? *planting seeds*
3. How did Mr. Farmer plant his seeds? *by scattering them with his hand*
4. What happened to the seeds that fell on the path? *Birds came and ate them.*
5. What happened to the seed that fell on the rocks? *They died because they didn't have water.*
6. What happened to the seeds that fell on the weeds? *The weeds choked them.*
7. What happened to the seeds that fell on good soil? *They grew and grew.*
8. Jesus said the seeds were like _____? *God's Word*
9. Who comes and steals God's Word from our hearts? *Satan*
10. Are you going to hear and listen to God's Word?

My Ears Belong to Jesus

Chapter 6
My Eyes Belong to Jesus

Memory Verse

I lift up my eyes to you. Psalm 123:1

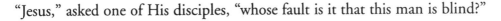

Story to Share
I Can See!

Jesus and His disciples were walking in Jerusalem when they saw a blind man. Men who were blind couldn't work, so they sat by the road to beg for money.

"Jesus," asked one of His disciples, "whose fault is it that this man is blind?"

"I'd like to know, too," said another disciple. "Was it his sins or the sins of his parents that caused this man to lose his sight?"

Jesus shook His head, "Neither, my friends. This man is blind for a reason. But it has nothing to do with sin. It is so God can be praised."

Jesus spat on the ground in front of Him. Mixing his spit with the dusty dirt, Jesus made a mud mixture. He bent down and picked up the cool mud in his hands. Then Jesus put the mud over the man's eyes.

"Go," he told the blind man. "Wash your eyes in the Siloam pool."

The blind man obeyed Jesus. Eagerly he washed his eyes, wondering what this meant. When the mud was gone, he brushed as much water from his eyes as he could. "I can see," he said, "I can see. Once I was blind and couldn't see but now I can see."

The blind man thanked Jesus for giving him the joy of sight. He never wanted to use his eyes to see things that were wrong. He wanted to see Jesus and the other miracles He did. He wanted to watch Jesus as He taught the crowds. His eyes belonged to Jesus!

— based on John 9:1-12

Questions for Discussion
1. Does Jesus love us even if we are blind or we can't hear or walk?
2. When Jesus helps us what should we do?

• • • • • • • • • • •

Materials
- blinded eyes pattern
- poster board
- scissors

Directions
1. Before class, duplicate the blinded eyes for each child on poster board.
2. Give each student a blinded eyes piece.
3. Demonstrate the verse to the children and have them do it with you.

Usage
You may use two-sided tape to lightly tape the eyes to the children's faces. They will enjoy taking off the eyes to lift theirs up to God.

My Eyes Belong to Jesus

Memory Verse Motion

I   *point to self*
Lift up my eyes   *remove blinded eyes; lift eyes toward heaven*
to you.   *point to heaven*
Psalm 123:1   *hold up right hand, 1-2-3 fingers;*
               hold up left hand and 1 finger

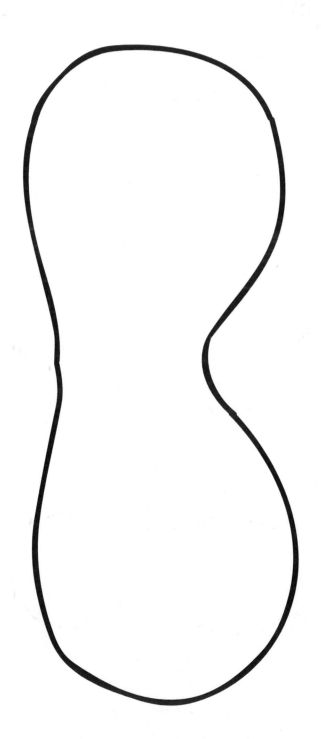

Lifted-Up Eyes

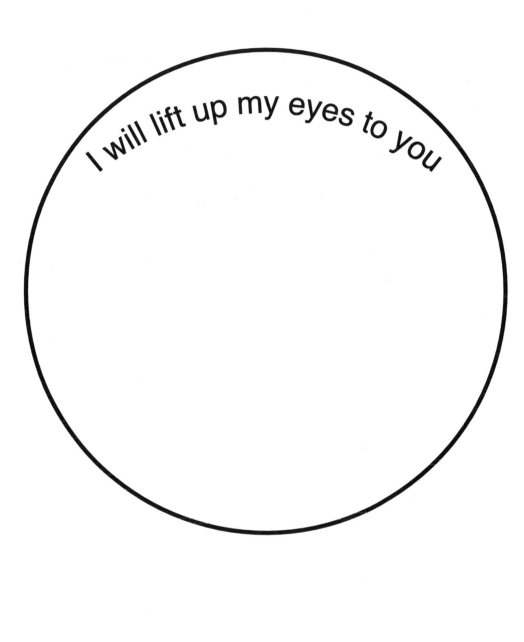

I will lift up my eyes to you

activity

Materials

- eyes and verse
- chenille wire
- plastic margarine lids
- large wiggle eyes
- glue
- clear tape

Directions

1. Before class, cut the lids to the size of the verse circle. Duplicate and cut out one circle and set of eyes per child.
2. Show how to poke a chenille wire through the middle of the verse circle until $1/2$" is showing through the back. Have them bend the wire until it is flat on the circle.
3. Help them glue the circle to the lid.
4. Show how to wrap the wire around a finger and remove it so it stays curled.
5. Allow the children to glue the wiggle eyes to the paper eyes then tape them to the free end of the chenille wire.

Usage

Say, **Our verse today is a prayer to God. Why do you think you should keep your eyes on Jesus?** Allow time for the children to respond. Say, **If you keep your eyes on Jesus, you won't see and desire worldly pleasures. You will want to belong to Jesus.**

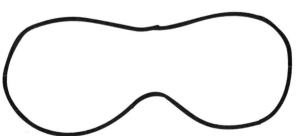

My Eyes Belong to Jesus

59

craft

Sunglasses Holder

Materials

- dishwashing soap bottles, 1 qt. size
- scissors
- label
- crayons
- ribbon
- glue

Directions

1. Before class, cut the tops off the bottles, leaving 5" at the bottom. Duplicate and cut out one label for each child. Use some of the ribbon to make bows.
2. Allow the children to color the label.
3. Instruct the students to glue the label to the front of the bottle.
4. Demonstrate how to glue the ribbon around the top of the label and a bow in the middle.
5. Say, **You can use this for your sunglasses or you can give it to someone else for their sunglasses. Sunglasses may shield our eyes from the sun, but we should always keep our eyes on God.**

My Eyes Belong to Jesus

I lift up my eyes to you.
Psalm 123:1

One Green Frog

craft / activity

● ● ● ● ● ● ● ● ● ●

Materials
- frog mask
- large rubber bands
- stapler
- clear tape
- crayons

Directions
1. Before class, duplicate the frog mask for each child and cut out the eyes and mouths on the dashed lines. Cut the rubber bands so each is one long band. Staple the bands to the sides of the frog faces. Cover the staples with tape to avoid injury.
2. Allow the children to color a frog face.
3. Help the children to put on their masks.
4. Say, **This poem is about a frog that saw Jesus heal the blind man. What else do you think he saw that day?** Demonstrate how they should roll their eyes and stick out their tongues as you say the poem.

My Eyes Belong to Jesus

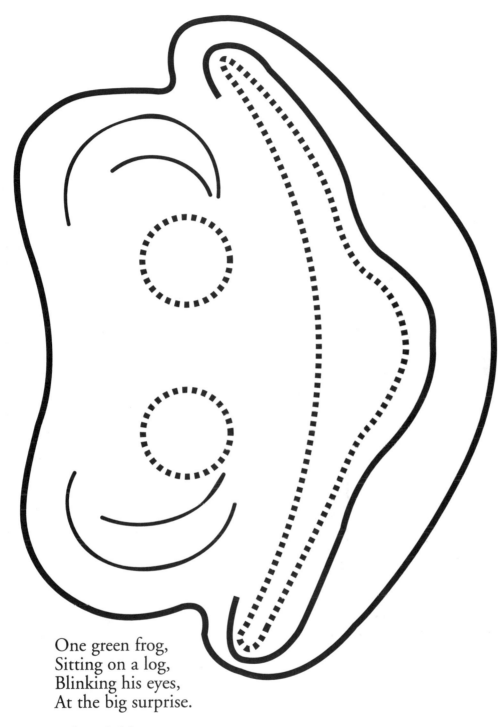

One green frog,
Sitting on a log,
Blinking his eyes,
At the big surprise.

What did he see,
Oh what could it be?
The blind man's eyes,
Were his surprise!

Why were the eyes,
The frog's surprise?
'Cause they could see,
As well as can be!

61

I See You!

craft / snack

. . . .

Materials
- face pattern
- clear, self-stick plastic
- crayons
- round crackers
- soft cream cheese
- grapes
- plastic knives

Directions
1. Before class, duplicate one face per child. Cut the grapes in half.
2. Allow the children to color the face.
3. Assist them in writing their names on the back and in using the self-stick plastic to cover both sides of the face.
4. Demonstrate how to spread the cream cheese on the crackers and put a grape half in the middle.
5. Show the children how to place the cracker eyes on their face placemat. Ask, **Is your man seeing like the man Jesus healed?**

My Eyes Belong to Jesus

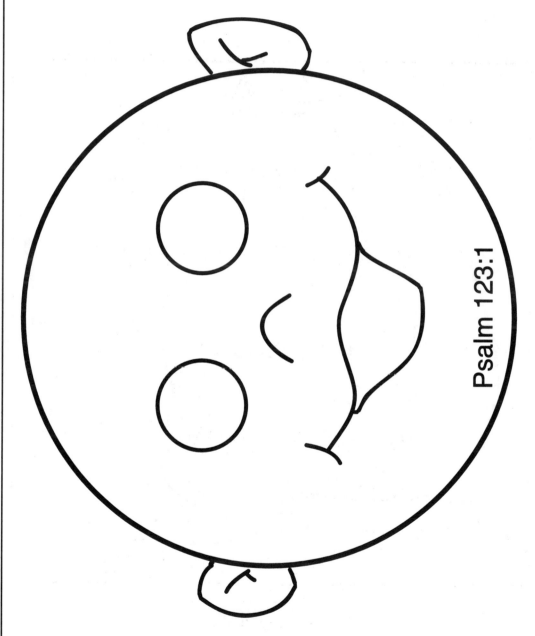

Psalm 123:1

Blinded Eyes Healed

activity

Materials
- activity sheet
- scissors
- glue
- crayons

Directions
1. Before class, duplicate and cut out one set of eyes per student. Duplicate the picture of the blind man for each child.
2. Show the children where to glue the eyes to the blind man.
3. Allow them to color the picture.

Usage
Ask, What do you think would have happened to the blind man if he had decided not to obey Jesus when He said, "Go wash your eyes in the Siloam pool?" Do you think he was glad he obeyed God?

craft

Materials
- flower plaque
- crayons
- construction paper
- glue
- silk flowers
- hole punch
- yarn

Directions
1. Before class, duplicate the picture for each student.
2. Say, **Think of all the beautiful things your eyes show you. Let's say this thank-You prayer to God:**
   Thank-You, God, that I can see. *point to eyes*
   The beautiful world You made for me. *point to self*
3. Allow the children to color the flower plaque.
4. Show how to glue the plaque on the construction paper.
5. Show where to glue on the flowers.
6. Punch two holes at the top of each plaque and tie yarn through it for a hanger.

My Eyes Belong to Jesus

Thank You, God

Beautiful Sights!

puzzle

· · · · · · · · · · ·

Materials
- activity sheet
- small wiggle eyes
- glue
- crayons

Directions
1. Say, **Look at the beautiful flowers! If you look closely at the activity sheet, you can see five animals looking at you.**
2. Instruct the students to glue the wiggle eyes to the animals they find and to then color the page.

Usage
It would be helpful to count out the ten eyes and put them in film cases or other small containers for each student. Make sure you have extras for lost eyes!

I lift up my eyes to you.
Psalm 123:1

Chapter 7
My Things Belong to Jesus

Memory Verse

The earth is the Lord's, and everything in it. Psalm 24:1

Story to Share
They're Mine!

Simon had everything a young man could want. His father was very rich and Simon knew he would inherit it all some day. He was also being trained to become a religious leader. But Simon felt sad in his heart. There was something missing from his life.

I know, thought Simon. *I'll go ask Jesus. He knows the answer to every question.* When Simon found out where Jesus was, he ran up to Him. Kneeling and bowing his head, Simon asked, "Lord, what must I do to get to Heaven? I want to live forever."

Jesus said, "Simon, you need to follow the commandments of God."

Simon nodded. "I have, Jesus. I have kept the commandments since I have been a small boy and knew what I was doing."

Jesus took Simon's hand and pulled him to his feet. "Then there is just one thing more you must do," Jesus said.

"Tell me, Jesus," said Simon. "I'll do whatever You say."

Jesus knew Simon meant what he was saying, but Jesus also knew that Simon loved the things that his money bought. Jesus knew that Simon's possessions were important to him.

Jesus said, "If you want to live forever with Me in heaven, Simon, you must sell all that you have and give your money to the poor."

Simon stared at Jesus. "But they're mine," he said. "The things I have are mine!"

"Are they more important than Me, Simon?" asked Jesus.

Without a word, Simon turned and walked away. He wouldn't give his things to Jesus.

— based on Luke 18:18-23

Questions for Discussion
1. What was the first thing Jesus told Simon he must do to get to Heaven?
2. Should you obey the commandments in the Bible?

game

Materials
- world and money patterns
- scissors
- crayons
- craft sticks
- glue
- 8-oz. coffee cans

Directions
1. Before class, duplicate and cut out a set of patterns for each child.
2. Allow the children to color the patterns.
3. Show how to glue the world to the front of the coffee can.
4. Distribute the money and craft sticks.
5. Show how to glue each piece of money to a craft stick to weight it.
6. Demonstrate how to stand over the can and drop the money into the can.

Usage
This is a great way to teach the memory verse. Say, **The earth is the Lord's** while the child is getting ready to drop the money in the can. Say, **and everything in it** as the money goes in the can.

I Got It In!

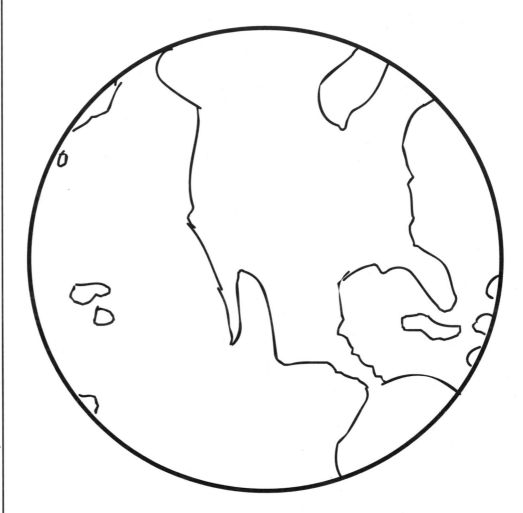

Hidden Toys

puzzle

· · · · · · · · · ·

Materials
- activity sheet
- crayons

Directions
1. Before class, duplicate the activity sheet for each child.
2. Say, Some things that may be important to you are hidden in the picture. Find a car, truck, toothbrush, doll, purse, teddy bear, teapot and dog. Then find who should be the most important of all. Who is He?

My Things Belong to Jesus

activity

Materials
- two cups of flour
- two cups cornstarch
- one cup of colored glue
- waxed paper
- resealable plastic bags
- label pattern

Directions
1. Before class, combine the flour, cornstarch and glue until dough forms. If dry, add water until the dough is soft and easy to form. Duplicate the label for each child.
2. Give each child a piece of waxed paper and a bit of the dough. Say, **Think of the toy you like best. Would you be willing to give it to Jesus if He asked for it?**
3. Allow the children to make a model of their favorite toy with the dough.
4. Show them how to glue the label on a plastic bag so they can take their dough home with them.

All I Have

You can have it, Jesus

You can have it, Jesus

Walking Away from Jesus

puzzle

. . . .

Materials
- activity sheet
- crayons

Directions
1. Before class, duplicate the activity sheet for each child.
2. Provide crayons for the children to trace the path in the maze.

Discuss
Say, The rich, young man wasn't willing to give up the things his money bought for him. Do you think his trip home was happy? Do you think he made the right choice? Can you help the young man find his way from Jesus back to his big house and all the things it held?

Usage

Sing the song to the tune of "Yankee Doodle" while doing the motions. This is a good activity for when the wiggles start to get the best of your class!

You Won't Be Sorry

Verse One

1. A young man came to Jesus,
   walk in place

2. How can I get to heaven?
   hands out, palms up

3. He didn't like what Jesus said,
   shake head

4. So said good-bye and left Him.
   wave good-bye

Verse Two

1. Everything belongs to God,
   arms out to form circle

2. The earth and all that's in it.
   left arm still out, right motions down in circle

3. So gladly give your things to Him,
   offer things to Jesus

4. You won't be sad— not one bit!
   shake head with big smile

They're Mine!

Materials
- activity sheet
- crayons

Directions
1. Before class, duplicate the activity sheet for each child.
2. Say, Jesus wants us to enjoy the things we have. But He knew they were too important to the rich, young man. Jesus wants to come first in our lives.
3. Say, Here are some things you may have at home. Color the two toys in each group which are exactly alike.

My Things Belong to Jesus

73

game

· · · · · · · · · · ·

Materials

• sequence cards
• scissors
• crayons

Directions

1. Before class, duplicate and cut out the sequence cards, one set per child.
2. Allow the children to color the cards.
3. Ask, **Can you remember the story? Which picture should come first?**
4. Continue helping the children as they need coaching through the first sequencing: young man coming to Jesus, Jesus saying to obey the commandments, Jesus saying one more thing: give up money, sad man leaving.
5. Instruct the students to mix up the cards and try again with a partner.

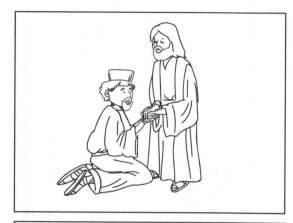

Story Sequence Cards

My Things Belong to Jesus

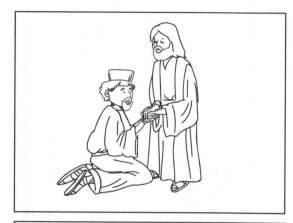

74

Sad, Young Man

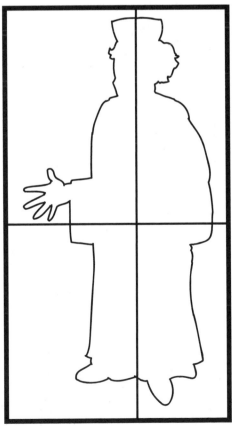

puzzle

· · · · · · · · · · ·

Materials
- activity sheet
- scissors
- glue
- crayons
- pennies

Directions
1. Before class, duplicate the puzzle pieces and cut out one set per child. Then duplicate the solid man pattern for each student.
2. Give each child a copy of the man shape and a set of puzzle pieces. Instruct the class to glue the pieces in the correct place on the solid man.
3. Say, **What was more important to this man than belonging to Jesus?** His money and the things his money could buy. Glue a penny in the man's hand to remind you not to be like this sad, young man.

My Things Belong to Jesus

Memory Verse

You will be my sons and daughters. 2 Corinthians 6:18

Story to Share
Samuel Hears God's Call

Samuel had a new home. He no longer lived with his mother, Hannah, and his father, Elkanah. Before Samuel was born, his mother had promised her baby to God if He would bless her with children. "I live in God's house," whispered Samuel in the quiet of his room. "I live in God's house with the priest, Eli."

Samuel loved his new home, and he loved doing his chores and learning the things that Eli taught him. There was joy in his heart because Samuel knew he was pleasing God.

One night, Samuel was sleeping on his tiny cot when he heard, "Samuel, Samuel." Rushing to Eli's room, Samuel said, "Eli, I heard you call. What can I do for you?"

"I didn't call you, son," said Eli.

Samuel went back to bed, but he wasn't sleeping long when he heard, "Samuel, Samuel." Again, Samuel ran to Eli. "Yes, Eli. Can I do something for you?" asked Samuel.

"What a dream you must be having, Samuel. Go back to bed," chuckled Eli.

When Samuel ran to Eli the third time, Eli understood what was happening. "Samuel, the Lord is calling you," he told him. "The next time you hear Him call, answer, 'Speak, Lord, I am listening.'"

Samuel snuggled down into his bed, and again he heard, "Samuel, Samuel." This time Samuel was ready. "Speak, Lord, I am listening," he said.

"Samuel," said the Lord. "I want to speak through you to My people. Will you give yourself to Me?"

"Yes," Samuel said eagerly. "I will be Your servant and give my life to You."

— based on 1 Samuel 3:1-21

Questions for Discussion
1. Was Samuel quick to obey even when he thought Eli was calling?
2. Do you have trouble obeying when someone calls you?

Samuel's Yes

Materials

- tag
- scissors
- spring-type clothespins
- blankets

Directions

1. Before class, duplicate and cut out the tags, then glue them to the clothespins.
2. Pin the tags on the actors.
3. Place blankets on the floor for Samuel and Eli.

Usage

Your students will not be able to read this script, but they will catch on fast if you go through it once. Everyone will want to have a chance to participate so plan enough time for all to have a turn.

My Life Belongs to Jesus

Skit

God's voice: Samuel, Samuel!

Samuel: *runs to Eli*
  Here I am, Eli.

Eli: Go back to bed.

God's voice: Samuel, Samuel!

Samuel: *runs to Eli*
  Here I am, Eli.

Eli: Go back to bed.

God's voice: Samuel, Samuel!

Samuel: *runs to Eli*
  Here I am, Eli.

Eli: God is calling you.

God's voice: Samuel, Samuel!

Samuel: I belong to You, God.

SAMUEL

ELI

GOD

Sons and Daughters

craft

Materials

- paper dolls and clothes
- scissors
- crayons
- file folders
- letter-size envelopes
- glue

Directions

1. Before class, duplicate and cut out the dolls and clothes, one set per child.
2. Allow the children to color them.
3. Instruct the students to glue a child on each half of the folder, leaving room on the bottom right for an envelope.
4. Show where to glue the envelope at the bottom of the folder so the pocket remains open.
5. Instruct the students to keep the clothes in the envelope.
6. To use, lay the folder flat and lay the clothes on the boy and girl. When finished, the folder may be closed for a handy carrying case.

Usage

As the children dress their boy and girl say, **Dress your boy and girl,** then we'll say to them the Words of God, "You will be my sons and daughters."

My Life Belongs to Jesus

Here's My Life

Materials
- activity sheet
- crayons

Directions
1. Before class, duplicate the activity sheet for each child.
2. Say, These boys and girls want to give their lives to Jesus, but they're all tangled up. Use a crayon to follow the paths and untangle them.

My Life Belongs to Jesus

80

A Wise Girl and Boy

A wise girl gives her heart to Jesus Christ.
A wise girl gives her heart to Jesus Christ.
A wise girl gives her heart to Jesus Christ.
God's daughter she becomes.

A wise boy gives his heart to Jesus Christ.
A wise boy gives his heart to Jesus Christ.
A wise boy gives his heart to Jesus Christ.
Then God's son he becomes.

Will you give your heart to Jesus Christ?
Will you give your heart to Jesus Christ?
Will you give your heart to Jesus Christ?
Become His fam-i-ly.

craft/song

• • • • • • • • • • •

Materials
• heart
• red poster board
• scissors
• glue
• lace
• sequins

Directions
1. Before class, duplicate and cut out a heart for each child from red poster board. Write the memory verse on each one.
2. Allow the children to decorate their hearts with glue, lace and sequins.
3. Sing the song to the tune of "The Wise Man Built His House Upon the Rock." On the first verse have the girls stand up and hold their hearts up; the second verse the boys; the third verse all those who want to give their life to Jesus.

My Life Belongs to Jesus

81

game

Materials

- game board and cards
- scissors
- crayons (optional)
- clear, self-stick plastic (optional)

Directions

1. Before class, duplicate and cut out one game board per child and a set of cards. You may color the cards and cover them with self-stick plastic, if desired.
2. Form a circle on the floor with the children and give each child a game board.
3. Place all of the cards upside-down in the middle of the circle.
4. Pick a player and instruct the player to pick a card. If it matches one of that player's squares on his or her board, it may be placed on the board. If it does not, that player should place it on the bottom of the card stack. The next player then takes a turn. The first with three in a row wins.

Usage

Say, **God doesn't care where we live or what we look like. He wants us all to be His kids.** Note: If your class is large, form two circles.

My Life Belongs to Jesus

Jesus' Kids

Game Board

Cards

bulletin board

• • • • • • • • • • •

Materials
- picture of each student
- construction paper
- heart patterns
- lace
- fiberfill
- spray glitter

Directions
1. Before class, use the small heart pattern to cut various colors of hearts and attach them to the bulletin board for a border. Freehand or stencil the lettering at the top of the board as shown. Cut out one large heart for each child.
2. Instruct the children to glue their picture to the center of the heart.
3. Show the students how to glue lace along the edge of heart. Assist each child in putting his or her heart on the bulletin board.
4. Attach a poof of fiberfill "cloud" to the bottom of each heart.
5. Lightly spray glitter over the entire board.

My Life Belongs to Jesus

We Belong to Jesus

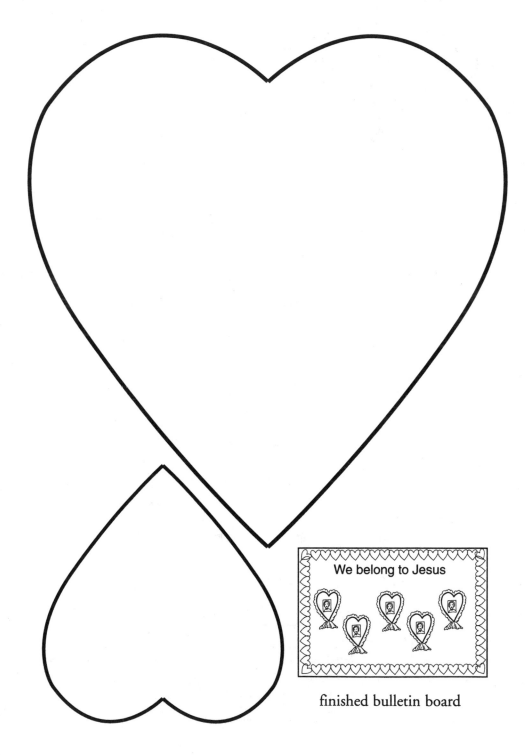

We belong to Jesus

finished bulletin board

Son or Daughter of God

craft

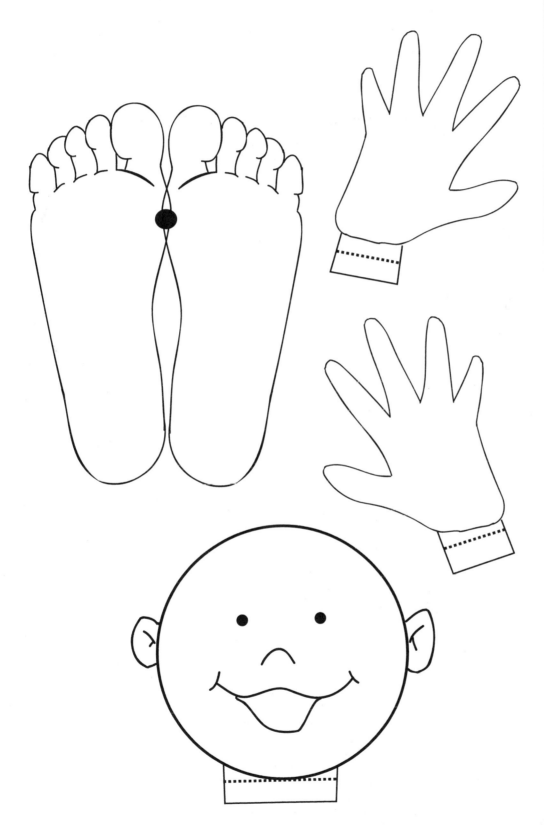

Materials
- feet, hands and face
- poster board
- balloons
- crayons
- glue

Directions
1. Before class, duplicate the feet, hands and face patterns on poster board for each child. Cut out the pieces and punch a hole in the center of the feet piece. Use a permanent marker to write on each balloon: My life belongs to Jesus.
2. Help each child blow up a balloon.
3. Allow the children to color the feet, hands and face.
4. Demonstrate how to put the knot of the balloon through the feet.
5. Show the children how to glue the hands to the side of the balloon and the head to the back.

My Life Belongs to Jesus

Chapter 9
Miscellaneous Activities

_____

has learned to
use his/her ears for listening.

_____   _____
(teacher)   (date)

_____

has learned to
make Jesus happy by sharing.

_____   _____
(teacher)   (date)

_____

can sing
praises to the Lord.

_____   _____
(teacher)   (date)

_____

knows how
to use his/her feet to obey.

_____ _____
(teacher)   (date)

_____

has very
helpful hands.

_____ _____
(teacher)   (date)

_____

has promised to
always live for Jesus.

_____ _____
(teacher)   (date)

Snacking on Me

snack

. . . .

Materials

- frame pattern
- ginger snap cookies
- thin pretzel strips
- raisins

Directions

1. Before class, duplicate and cut out the frame for each child.
2. Give each child a ginger snap cookie head, pretzel strips for a body, and raisins for face, feet and hands.
3. Demonstrate how the students can "create" themselves with the food items.
4. Give the students the frame so they may draw a picture of the "person" they made — before they eat it! Ask, **Who belongs to Jesus?**
5. Other food items may be added for extra creativity: cereal for ears, red candy-coated chocolate for mouth, parsley for hair, etc.

Miscellaneous Activities

. . . .

Materials

- card patterns
- poster board
- scissors
- crayons or markers
- clear, self-stick plastic
- envelopes (optional)

Directions

1. Before class, duplicate two sets of cards on poster board, color them and cover them with clear, self-stick plastic for durability.

2. Say, **See if you can put all of the matching cards together. When you are done, stand and say, "I belong to Jesus."**

Usage

This is a good game for your "fast workers" who complete projects before the others. Allow the students to make their own Matching Review games to take home. Provide envelopes, which the children may also decorate, to hold the games.

Miscellaneous Activities

Matching Review

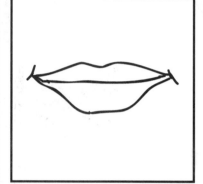

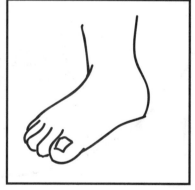

I Belong to Jesus Wreath

craft

• • • • • • • • • •

Materials
- plate center and decoration patterns from p. 92
- 9" paper plates
- glue
- ribbon
- crayons

Directions
1. Before class, duplicate and cut out the plate center and decoration patterns, one set per child. Tie the ribbon into bows, one per child.
2. Direct the students to glue the plate center in the middle of the back side of a paper plate.
3. Allow the students to color the wreath decorations.
4. Show how to glue the decorations around the wreath, leaving the bottom open for a bow.
5. Instruct the students to glue a bow to the bottom center of the plate.

Usage
The decorations may be added to the wreath each week to represent the lessons.

Miscellaneous Activities

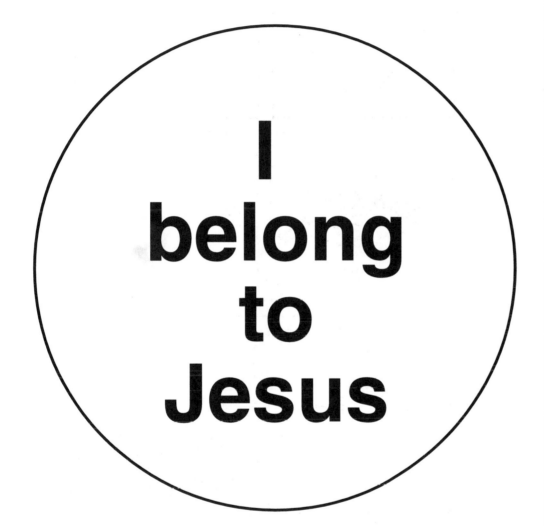

I belong to Jesus

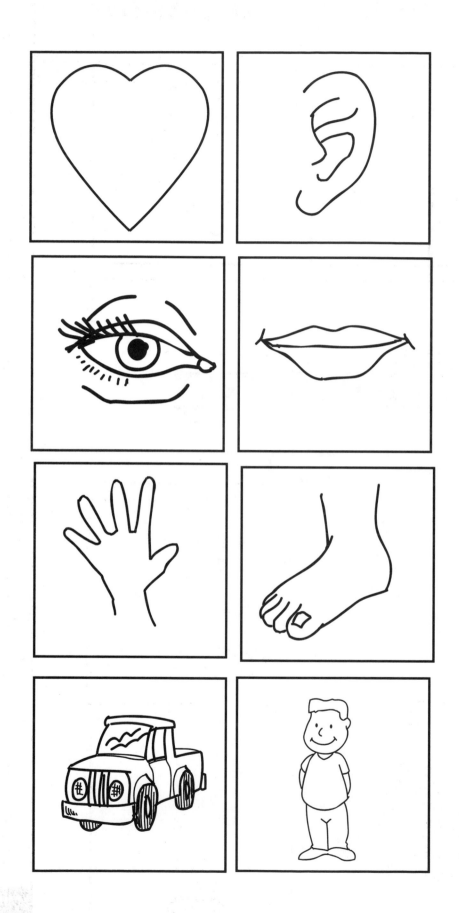

It Belongs to Jesus

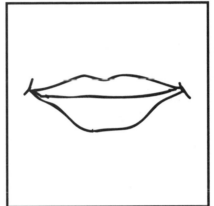

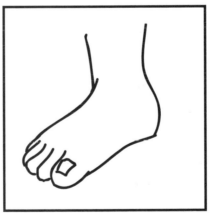

93

Materials

- game pieces
- spring-type clothespins
- glue
- paper lunch sack

Directions

1. Duplicate and cut out enough game pieces for each student plus two other sets.
2. Glue one set of game pieces on the clothespins. Put the other sets in the paper sack.
3. Clip a game piece on each child.
4. Line the children up against a wall.
5. Stand 10 feet away from the line and chose a game piece from the bag.
6. Say, **Hearts move forward two steps.** The hearts should say, "My heart belongs to Jesus," and move forward two steps. Place the heart back in the sack and choose another piece.
7. Continue until someone reaches a pre-designated finish line.

Miscellaneous Activities

craft

• • • • • • • • • • •

Materials

- symbol patterns
- paper grocery sacks
- scissors
- glue
- crayons
- craft sticks

Directions

1. Before class, duplicate and cut out one set of symbols per child. Cut the sides from a sack for each child. Cut a hole in the closed end for the head to fit through.
2. Allow the children to color the symbols.
3. Show where to glue the heart and assist in writing the child's name on the back. Other symbols may be glued on at random.
4. Have the children glue the "I Belong to Jesus" sign to a craft stick so it may be held.

Usage

This project is good for attendance. Glue on the heart on the first day of the unit. Then have the children add a new symbol each time they attend. Take a picture of the children in their jackets at the end of the unit or have them parade through the church.

Miscellaneous Activities

I Belong to Jesus Jacket

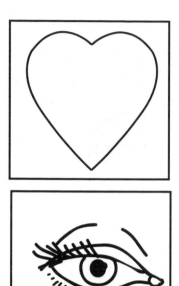

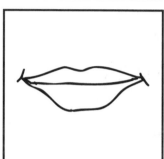

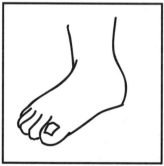

I belong to Jesus

Hurrah!

song

. . . .

Directions
1. Sing song to the tune of "The Farmer in the Dell."
2. Demonstrate the motions as you sing the song, then ask the students to join you.

Verse 1:
My heart belongs to God,
My heart belongs to God,

cover heart

I'll sing aloud and shout,
HURRAH, because
My heart belongs to God.

punch fist in air

Verse 2:
My hands belong to God...

hold out hands

Verse 3:
My feet belong to God...

march in place

Verse 4:
My mouth belongs to God...

point to mouth

Verse 5:
My ears belong to God...

pull out ears

Verse 6:
My eyes belong to God...

roll eyes around

Verse 7:
My things belong to God...

hold out clothes

Verse 8:
My life belongs to God...

arms outstretched

Full Hearts

craft

Materials

- 6" paper plates
- large heart, small heart and activity sheet
- red construction paper
- scissors
- stapler
- clear tape
- glue
- craft sticks
- crayons

Directions

1. Before class, duplicate and cut out one large heart from red paper and one small heart and set of symbols per child.
2. Give each child a paper plate and a half of a plate. Assist in stapling the two together — right sides together— to make a pocket. Cover the staples with tape to avoid injury.
3. Give the students a large heart and instruct them to glue it to the half plate, then glue the small heart to the middle of the large heart.
4. Allow the students to color the other items, then instruct them to glue them to the ends of craft sticks.
5. Each class time, the stick which goes with the lesson may be added to the heart pocket.

Miscellaneous Activities

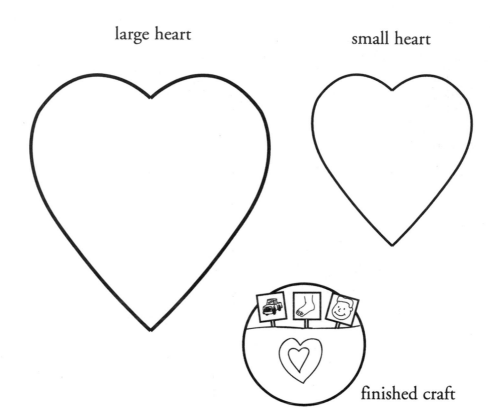

large heart   small heart

finished craft

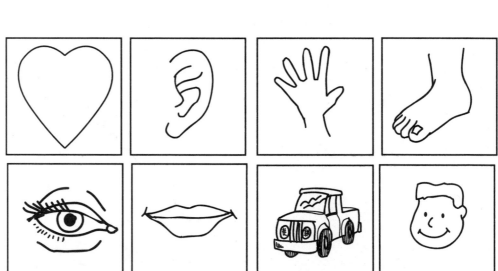

symbols

96